Sand Creatures and Castles

SAND CREATURES AND CASTLES

How To Build Them
Illustrated with line drawings and photographs

Bob and Pat Reed

Holt, Rinehart and Winston / New York

To Sara and David.

Printed in the United States of America
Designed by Robert Reed
10 9 8 7 6 5 4 3 2 1

Library of Congress Cataloging in Publication Data

Reed, Bob.
Sand creatures and castles.

SUMMARY: A guide for creating such sand sculptures at the beach
as animals, a car, and castles.
1. Sand sculpture—Juvenile literature. [1. Sand
sculpture. 2. Handicraft] I. Reed, Pat, joint author.
II. Title.
TT916.R43   731.4′2   75–32250
ISBN 0–03–014366–7

Photographs, pp. 52, 56 and 62,
New York Public Library Picture Collection
Photographs, p. 21, Counsellor Photos
Photographs, p. 24, Senior Studios
All other photographs, Jay J. Smith

Contents

Introduction

Sculpting in the sand

Sand of the right consistency can be shaped much like clay. In some ways, it is better. Sand and water are available in large quantities at the beach and, from an ecological point of view, you aren't wasting a natural resource—just altering its shape for awhile. The one drawback to sculpting sand at the beach is that your creation is not permanent. It will disappear with the next high tide. But this realization should help you not to worry about perfection. Satisfaction comes in making something with your hands. It's "art for art's sake." The fun is in the doing.

Sand sculpting is an ideal family activity. Each family member from the eldest to the youngest can be involved in the project and have a full share of the fun and sense of achievement. Those who are so inclined can draw the outline and do the modeling; the hands of others can be used for shoveling sand and fetching and sprinkling water.

Sand sculpture contests have become very popular on both coasts and on many lake shores. In Ocean City, New Jersey, which claims to be "America's Greatest Family Resort," there are two sand-sculpting contests every summer. In each, over a hundred eager sculptors in five age-related categories compete with such entries as a scale model of the Parthenon, a beagle, Rip Van Winkle, and a host of other creatures whose natural habitat is water: sea serpents, hippos, and whales. The prizes are nominal; the reward is the fun of planning and building the sculpture and the satisfaction of completing and admiring it. The local newspaper takes pictures of the winners and their sculptures before the high tide rolls in.

Many people are afraid they don't have the talent; yet, sand sculpture does not require artistic ability. The purpose of this book is to encourage those who would like to try sand sculpting but are uncertain how to go about it. Some people will be more successful than others, but almost anyone can be a sculptor in the sand.

The tools

The tools for sand sculpting can be as simple as a pail and shovel, or they can include other items you may have around the house and can easily carry to the beach, or molds that you can buy for under $1 where beach toys are sold. Here is a partial list, not including hands and fingers—which can be your most effective tools:

For shoveling
sand shovel (preferably metal)
small garden shovel (moves sand faster)
clam shell

For cutting
putty knife
trowel
table knife
shovel
egg-shaped
  stocking container
popsicle stick
clam shell

For molding and patting
back of shovel
rubber spatula

As molds

egg-shaped stocking container
tapered paper cups
plastic flowerpot
purchased plastic mold
funnel
sandpail

For decoration

shells, varied sizes and colors
sticks, straws
seaweed; beach grasses
feathers
small rake
whisk broom
  (for smoothing background)

Choosing the time and place

While there will be no such problem at a lake shore, those sculpting at the ocean front will be at the mercy of tides. Check the local tide tables. These are often posted each day at the entrance to the beach. If not, consult the local paper or the lifeguard. You will want to begin your sculpture some time after the water has reached its highest point and has begun to recede. Start long enough before the next high tide so that you can work leisurely, allowing yourself time for a swim and even lunch. It might take anywhere from one to four hours to complete the sculptures illustrated in this book, depending on their size and detail. A turtle (see p. 36) can be made in one hour, but the sphinx (p. 34) might take two hours or more. It's up to you.

If you feel hesitant about sculpting in full view of others, choose an isolated part of the beach. Or, if the tide is right at that time, wait until most of the people have gone for the day. However, there is no reason to be inhibited at the beach. Everyone is busy relaxing. No one cares what anyone else is doing. On the other hand, you might like to make some new friends. In that case, sand sculpting is a sure way to attract people and even their help . . . if you want it.

The chief factor in sand sculpting is choosing the right sand to work with. Avoid the dry, powdery sand and also sand that is only slightly damp. Choose a spot near the water where the sand is wetter. Test it first to make sure it's the right consistency—not too dry and not too wet. Take some in your hands. Form

it into a small ball. Does the shape hold? Does the sand retain the shape of a mold? If so, this is a good place to stake out your plot.

For best results, a summer morning is ideal. The sand is still cool and damp.

How to begin?

Sculpture is three-dimensional—it has width, depth, and height. You may realize, as you begin to sculpt, that you don't really know what a particular creature or castle might look like from *all* sides. It will help to have drawings of the subject before you.

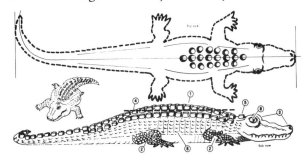

If you take this book to the beach, take along some transparent plastic wrap, make a little sand stand, cover the page with plastic, weight it down with a clam shell, and proceed. You can also make a copy or trace the desired pages and leave the book at home.

Choose what you would like to sculpt. If you are a beginner, choose a simple shape to start with, such as a snail or a turtle. You will be pleased with the results in less than an hour. You will also have gained experience in techniques that you will need to make more complicated sculptures later.

Be sure to study the pictures before you begin. Consult them as you go along. They are your guide to successful sculptures. Follow the instructions and illustrations closely until you gain confidence. For extra fun, try making caricatures by exaggerating some of the creatures' more prominent features—the dinosaur's armor plating, the alligator's fierce mouth, or the frog's bulging eyes.

A "Tool Guide" is provided with each set of instructions. If a tool is crossed out, you probably won't need it. You will, however, need the remaining ones. Whatever you do, don't give up for lack of a tool. Improvise with something you have.

The instructions are necessarily brief. If, as you go along, you want more information, refer back to the Introduction for a more detailed description of a technique. "Suggested sizes" are only suggestions. They indicate the width and height at the widest and highest parts of a creature. If you change one dimension, be sure to change the others to keep your sculpture in proportion.

The order of the sculpturing steps is most important:

1. **Lay out the length.**
2. **Make the outline.**
3. **Mound the general shape.**
4. **Pat entire figure smooth and firm.**
5. **Add the features.**
6. **Undercut around the base to "separate"** creature from the sand.

Making an outline

You have chosen the place. The sand is right. The picture is before you. Now you must decide how large your sculpture will be. Do you want your alligator to be four feet or twelve feet long? It will help to draw a "grid" on the sand. With something sharp—the edge of a shovel, a stick, or even your finger or toe—draw a line where the alligator's snout will be. Walk off the chosen length and, at the other end, draw a parallel line for the tip of its tail. A line down the center of these two, joining them, will help you to make the body symmetrical. Look at the drawing. The broken lines are the general outline or silhouette of the creature or castle as seen from above.

Now make your outline in the sand. If you aren't satisfied the first time, "erase" it and do it over.

To mound or sculpt in relief?

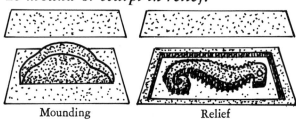

Mounding   Relief

When you have the basic outline, decide whether your sculpture will be mounded or in relief. In either case, the next step is the same—define your area from the surrounding sand. Dig the sand out to a depth of two–six inches all around your outline. For a mounded sculpture, pile the removed sand up onto the design, creating a three-dimensional bulk (see "beetle," p. 14). For a "relief" sculpture, shovel the sand away, keeping the creature in profile, lying on its side (see seahorse, p. 28).

Mounding

Use a shovel to mound up the sand. You can even kick it and pat it into place with your foot. As you are building up bulk, do not smooth too much. Loose sand will adhere to loose sand better than it will to a smooth, hard surface. Sand piled on itself to a height of several feet will tend to become conical in shape. To achieve a blocklike form, build to a height of a foot, stop, flatten the top, then continue to build

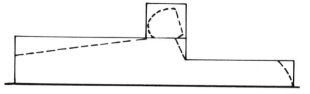

up your block. Repeat until the desired height is reached.

As you work, consult the drawings to make sure that the sand is taking on the correct proportions. For example, a sitting frog's head will be much higher than its hind legs.

Basic steps in sand sculpting

Mark off length

Draw an outline

Clear sand from outline

Begin mounding

Modeling techniques

When you have achieved the bulk you want, begin to mold or model the sand just as you would clay. Add water as needed and pack it down by patting the sand with the palms of your hands or the back of a shovel. Use a circular motion of your hands to mold the shape into contours. Don't worry about details at this point; concentrate on getting the general shape. Step back every once in awhile for a critical look. Work "in the round" rather than on one side at a time. You are creating something which has three dimensions. Walk around your sculpture to make sure you have the proportions and general shape right.

Keeping the sand moist

As you work, you will find completed areas are drying out, especially if you are building something large; sprinkle water now and then to keep the sand damp. (*Caution*: Poured water might destroy the shape you have achieved.) Pay special attention to the parts of the mound you will be cutting away later to achieve a particular shape. On the areas where you will be etching in surface features, add water and pat down gently to create a firm base.

Gluing

A small amount of wet sand added around certain features (e.g., the walrus's tusks, p. 38) will "glue" them in place whereas gravity might prevent them from sticking.

Pressing

This technique is used to add raised features, such as the ridges on a seahorse. Sand should be wet, but not so wet as for gluing, above. Mold with your hands. To make narrow, higher ridges, gently press the sand between your hands, first on one side, then on the other. This technique is also used to erect castle walls.

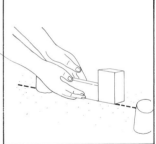

Cutting

Any tool with a sharp edge will cut away the sand, but something easy to control like a putty or table knife is best. The key to this activity is patience;

9

you don't want to cut away too much and then have to build it all up again. If you are doing a large, detailed sculpture, cut in or etch the details from the top down so that you won't drop sand on finished parts.

Etching in features

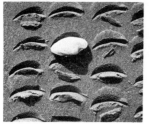

A putty knife, or stick, or a curved object like a clam shell, or half of an egg-shaped stocking container are good for etching in features.

Using molds

Molds must be treated carefully: Pack tightly with sand of claylike consistency, invert, and tap gently all around—especially on the top—then lift mold slowly, leaving the contoured sand in place.

Undercutting

Undercutting—meaning to cut away a little sand from underneath—is a special technique which allows parts of the creature to project from the sand. Interesting shadows are created, which add to the "realism." For example, when a turtle sits on the ground,

the edges of the bottom shell curve up. To achieve this effect, angle your tool downward, toward the base, then pull the sand out and away. After undercutting, if you want a rounded rather than a sharp edge, mold the area gently with wet fingers.

Technique for undercutting

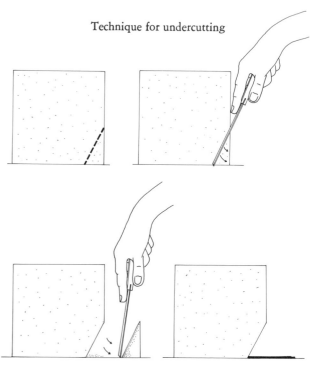

Words of caution

If you are using sharp tools, keep track of them so no one will be hurt by stepping on them. Make yourself a little sand yard for the tools and stick pointed ends in the sand when not in use. Don't use anything made of glass; it might break and be a hazard.

On the sand or of the sand

You can pretend that the sand background is either dry land or water. A turtle, snail, or car will rest on the "land." Other creatures will appear to be rising up out of the "water," like the hippo on p. 24 or the head of a shark (see p. 30). Later, when the high tide begins to swirl around your sculpture, the illusion of its being in the water will be heightened.

Decoration and special effects

Whale's eye

"Found" objects which are natural to the beach can be used as finishing touches for your sculpture.

Hair: seaweed or beach grasses

Horns: short straws or sticks

Eyes: shells—a small dark shell placed inside a larger white shell

Scales: shells, large and/or small in a symmetrical pattern

Teeth: broken clam shells; break the shells carefully so no one is hurt by flying fragments

Shading

"Coloring" can be achieved by wetting some of the features of your creature to make these areas darker than the rest. A sprinkling of powdery sand will lighten parts of your sculpture.

The boundary

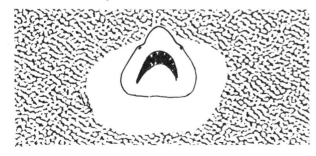

A boundary is useful, but it's more practical to wait until your sculpture is finished before you make it. A boundary will prevent bathers from accidentally walking into your sculpture. It will also serve to set off your creation, like a frame. Use a small rake or whisk broom to smooth the area around the finished sculpture.

Naming the baby

After the sculpture is finished and particularly if it is a creature you have become rather fond of, give it a name. Make the letters large enough. You can either write it in raised block letters or smooth the sand and etch the letters with your finger or a stick. The raised letters will be more dramatic and will photograph better. To make them uniform in size, make a square, level mound of sand for each one, then cut the letter out with a knife. Sprinkle powdery sand between the letters for contrast.

You might want a caption—"Do not feed"—or a title instead of a name. If you want your creature to "speak," draw a cartoon balloon around the words.

The proof is in the photo

Friends back home will never believe you unless you have a picture to prove that you really did make a fifteen-foot serpent or an open-jawed shark. Take a few pictures. Have the family or onlookers in one, to show the relative size of the sculpture. Try one without people, shooting upward from sand level, for an impressive photograph.

Above all, have fun at sand sculpting. The hints given here are intended as starting aids. You will soon have ideas of your own for other creatures and castles to be sculpted in the sand.

Alligator

Suggested size: 12 feet long, 2 feet wide, 18 inches high.

Distinguishing features: Eyes project above skull; upper teeth are exposed, giving the appearance of a "smile"; tip of snout is blunt; each leg has five claws; scales at sides and legs; armor plating on top.

Making the outline

Mark off length of alligator.
Draw an outline, including legs.
Clear sand from outline.
Begin mounding.

Sculpting the body

1) Mound sand up high between front and back legs, taper to snout and tail.
2) Mound up sand for legs.
3) With hands, add mounds of sand for bulges at end of snout and for eyes.
4) Flatten top; round sides and legs.

Adding the features

5) *Armor plating on top:* Use tapered soda cups as molds.
6) *Claws:* Add small shells.
7) *Eyes:* Push large white clam shells into eye bulges; into these, place small black mussel shells as *pupils.*
8) *Scales:* To create the pattern, use clam shell to indent and scoop away sand.
9) *Nostrils:* Insert mussel shells into snout. See front view.
10) *Mouth:* With sharp tool, etch outline all around snout. See front view.
11) *Upper teeth:* Slightly undercut bottom outline of mouth; insert clam shell shards (sharp, broken lengths) into upper mouth. See front view.

Final touches

Undercut all around.
Sprinkle powdery sand along lower sides (belly is lighter in color than top).

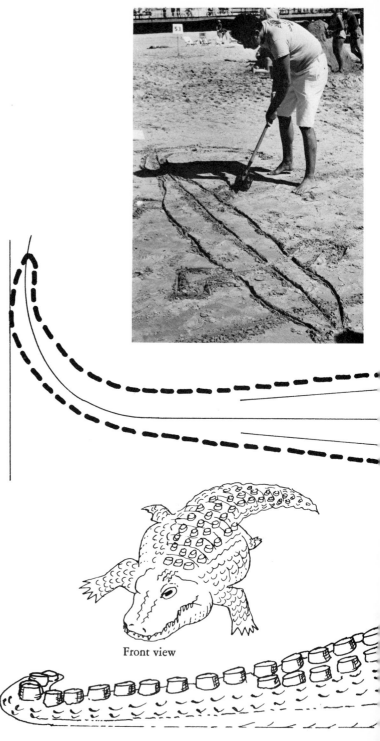

Front view

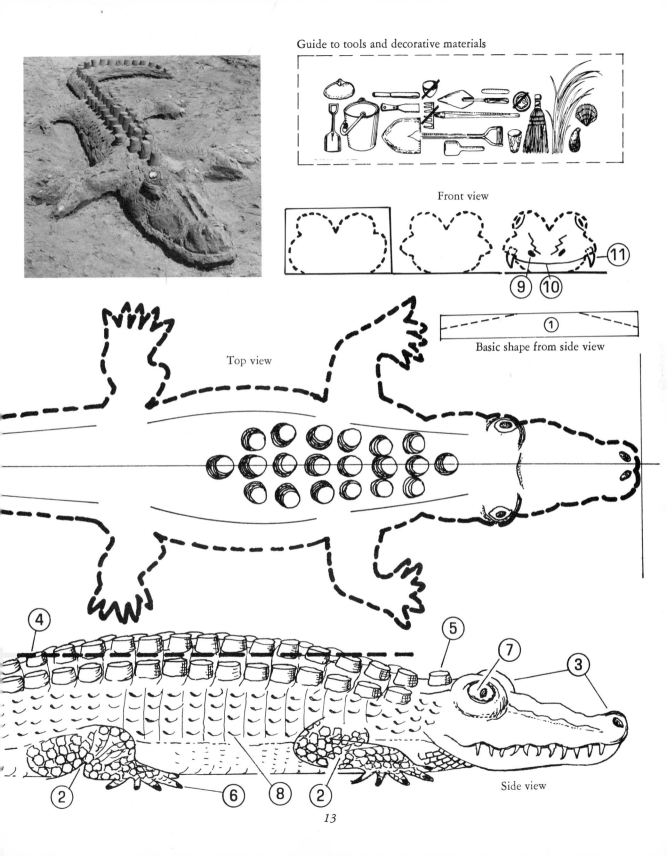

Guide to tools and decorative materials

Front view

Basic shape from side view

Top view

Side view

13

"Beetle"

Suggested size: 5 feet long, 3 feet wide, 3 feet high.

Distinguishing features: Two-door sedan; running boards; dual exhaust pipes.

Making the outline

Mark off length of car.
Draw an outline. See top view.
Clear sand from outline.
Begin mounding.

Sculpting the body

1) Mound up and firm semicircular shape. See drawing.
2) With shovel, cut away sand from front of arc for windshield and hood.
3) Etch in outline of fenders.
4) Remove sand at sides between front and back fenders, leaving a sand platform for running boards.
5) Cut away sand between back fenders to form engine lid, leaving a platform for rear bumper.

Adding the features

6) *Outlines for windows, doors, vents, hood, engine lid and front bumper:* All are etched in with putty knife.
7) *Door and hood handles:* With hands, mold and "glue" wet sand into place.
8) *Fender lights:* Mold wet sand into cone shapes on top of front fenders.
9) *Headlights:* Etch circles on front of fenders; mold ridges around circles.
10) *Taillights:* Mold and "glue" wet sand into place on rear fenders.
11) *Dual exhaust pipes:* "Glue" mounds of sand into place and mold to tubular shapes.
12) *Wheels:* Etch outline of wheels in fender area. Undercut to form wheels.
13) *Hubcaps:* Etch circles in centers.

Final touches

Undercut all around.
Make a license plate.
With hands, make rear tire tracks.
Add a stick to hood for radio antenna.

Guide to tools and decorative materials

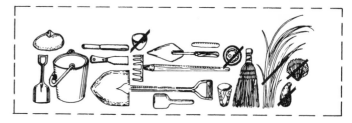

Basic shape from side view

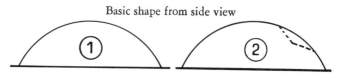

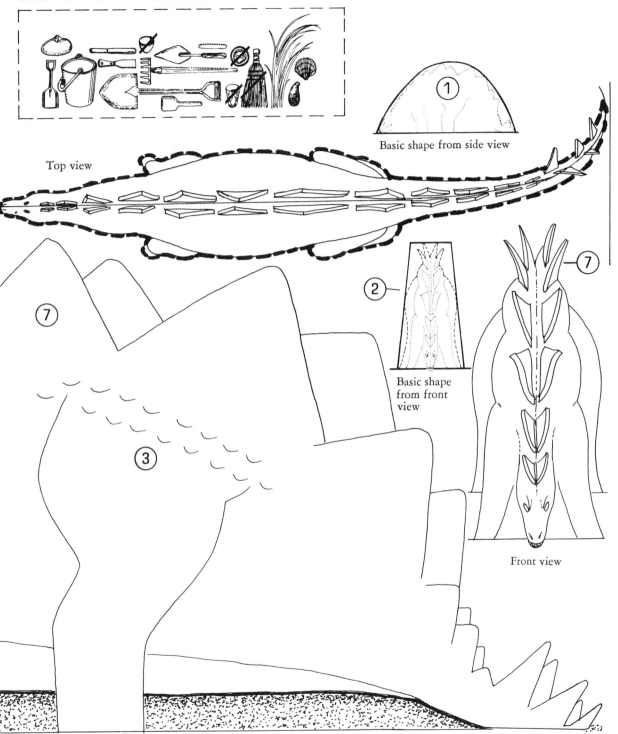

Guide to tools and decorative materials

Basic shape from side view

①

Top view

⑦

②

Basic shape from front view

⑦

③

Front view

Dog

Suggested size: 4 feet long, 18 inches wide, 18 inches high

Distinguishing features: Droopy jowls; large, floppy ears; sorrowful expression; bulbous nose; long, wide body; long, curving tail.

Making the outline

Mark off length of dog.
Draw an outline. See top view.
Clear sand from outline.
Begin mounding.

Sculpting the body

1) Mound up body to equal height and width.
2) Make humps for shoulders.
3) Slope front for head.
4) Mound up sand for front and rear legs.
5) Add sand to create curved tail. Pat and round entire figure.

Adding the features

6) *Head:* With hands, form dip between forehead and nose; make smooth.
7) *Jowls:* With sharp tool, shape curve of droopy jowls.
8) *Ears:* With sharp tool, etch outline; remove sand from front and above legs to put ear in relief; mold and round ears.
9) *Nose:* With hands, form small mound of sand; undercut nose to "raise" it above sand base; place mussel shell on tip.
10) *Eyes:* Press in mussel shells.
11) *Rear haunches:* With shovel or putty knife, shave sand down from top and haunches to form angle where they meet; firm.

Final touches

Undercut all around.
Rake all around.
With hands, form your dog's name in bone-shaped letters; make very smooth.

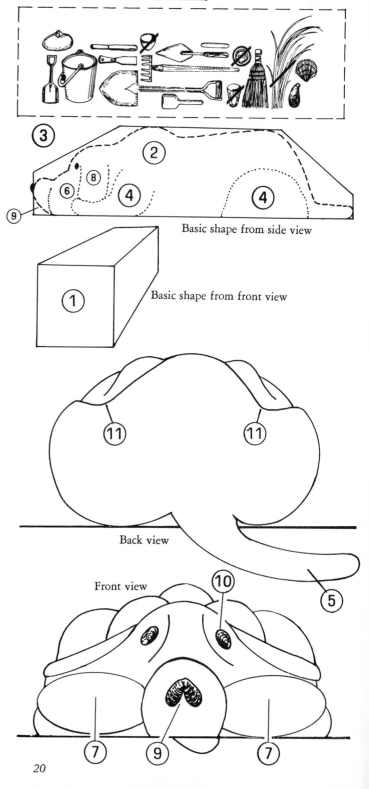

Guide to tools and decorative materials

Basic shape from side view

Basic shape from front view

Back view

Front view

20

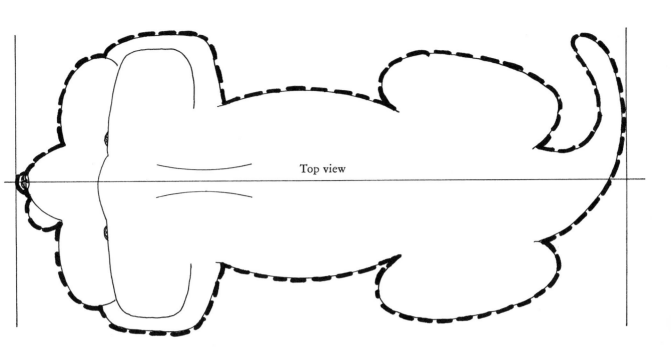

Top view

Frog

Suggested size: 3 feet long, 2 feet wide, 2 feet high.

Distinguishing features: Muscular rear legs; large, bulging eyes; wide, curved mouth; ridges along top of body.

Making the outline

Mark off length of frog.
Draw an outline. See top view.
Clear sand from outline.
Begin mounding.

Sculpting the body

1) Mound up sand to full height, tapering down back.
2) Mound up legs on either side; exaggerate construction and make absolutely smooth.
3) Use hands to make eye bulges; exaggerate size.
4) Make chest slope. *Caution:* Do not cut in too far or sand will crumble.

Adding the features

5) *Ridges on back:* By pressing sand between hands, make four–five ridges along back.
6) *Eyes:* Insert halves of egg-shaped stocking container or clam shells into eye bulges.
7) *Mouth:* With sharp tool, etch outline.
8) *Feet:* With sharp tool, form scalloped feet (five ridges).
9) *Rear legs:* With sharp tool, cut away sand to indicate separation between upper and middle leg; etch separation between middle and lower parts.

Final touches

Undercut all around.
Sprinkle powdery sand under mouth to lighten area.
Rake all around.

Guide to tools and decorative materials

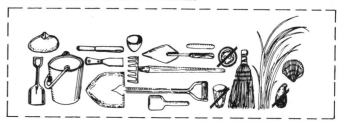

Front view

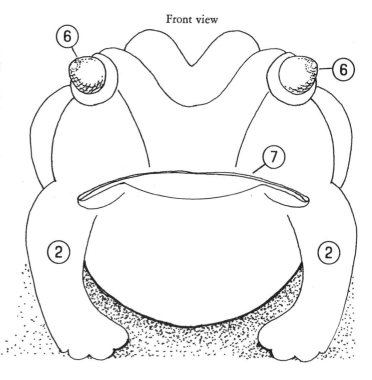

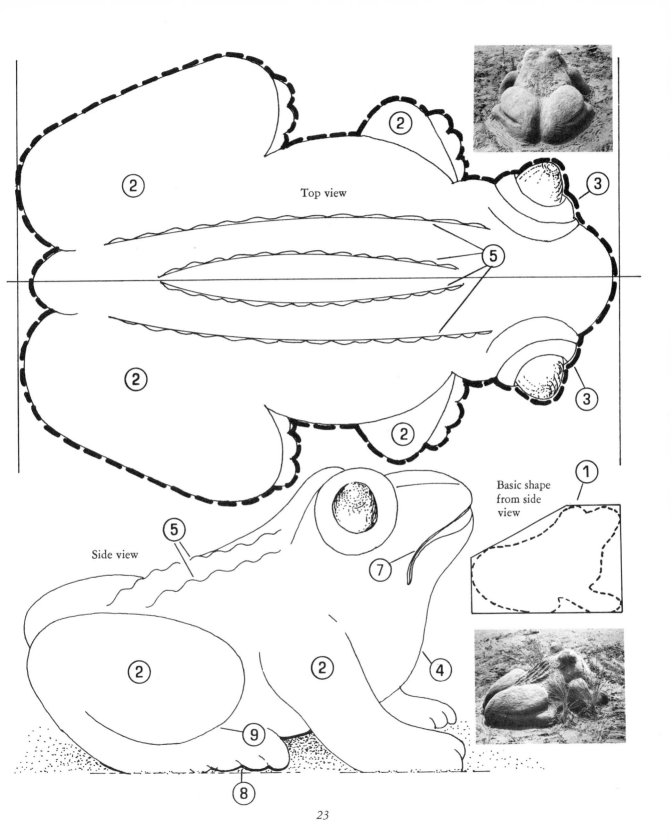

Top view

Side view

Basic shape
from side
view

Hippopotamus (in "water")

Suggested size: 4 feet long, 2 feet wide, 2 feet high.

Distinguishing features: Fat body with wrinkled skin; bulging eyes; large, open mouth; bristles on muzzle and ears; two large front teeth.

Making the outline

Mark off length of hippo.
Draw an outline. See top view.
Clear sand from outline.
Begin mounding.

Sculpting the body

1) Mound sand into shape shown in side view.
2) Shape legs at sides. Smooth and firm all over.
3) Add sand for head and mouth.
4) With shovel, cut away mouth; with hands, mold open mouth.
(*Note:* Lower jaw rests on sand.)

Adding the features

5) *Eyes:* On top of head, make two mounds the size of grapefruits. With wet sand, form two marble-sized *eyeballs* and place on top of eyes. Make small holes in eyeball centers for *pupils.*
6) *Ears:* With hands, form small, pointed ears.
7) *Nostrils:* Press in mussel shells.
8) *Bristles:* Add loose beach grass or straws to muzzle and ears.
9) *Teeth:* Using soda cups, mold two large teeth and place in lower jaw.
10) *Mouth:* With trowel or fingers, etch in details on roof of mouth.
11) *Wrinkled skin:* With trowel, etch in wrinkles and creases.
12) *Tail:* With hands, add ropelike tail; use grasses for bristles at end.

Final touches

Smooth all over.
Do not undercut; sand base becomes "water."
Add grasses for swampy appearance.

Guide to tools and decorative materials

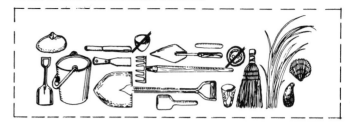

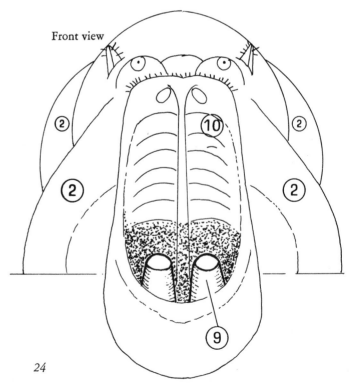

Front view

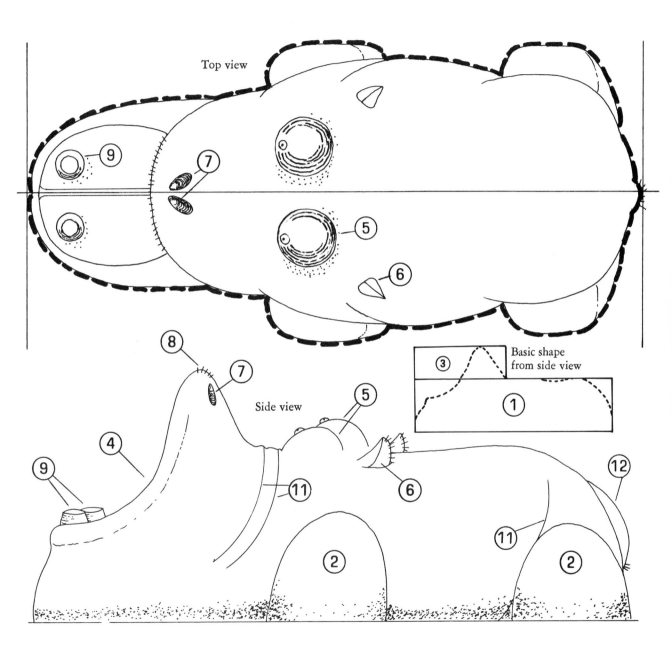

Top view

Side view

Basic shape from side view

Mermaid (from waist to fins)

Suggested size: at least two feet longer than model's legs.

Distinguishing features: Scales; curved shape; ridges in flared tail.

Making the outline

Model sits on sand as still as possible with legs outstretched.
Mark off length of fish half. See front view.
Draw an outline. See front view.
Clear sand from outline.
Begin mounding.

Sculpting the body

1) Begin mounding below the model's navel.
2) Mound up sand higher than model's legs and wider than hips, narrowing toward tail.
3) Mound up tail, rounding and smoothing all over.

Adding the features

4) *Scales* (from waist to flare of tail): Use shell or half of egg-shaped stocking container; press into sand and twist out. See photos.
5) *Scallops:* With putty knife, etch around scales.
6) *Ridges in tail:* Using sharp tool, etch lines as shown.

Final touches

Undercut all around.
Place small shell over model's navel.
Add grasses.
For a merman, add male model.

Guide to tools and decorative materials

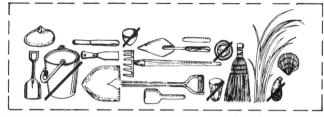

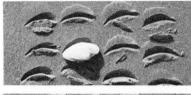

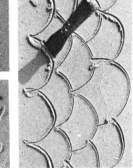

Making of scales

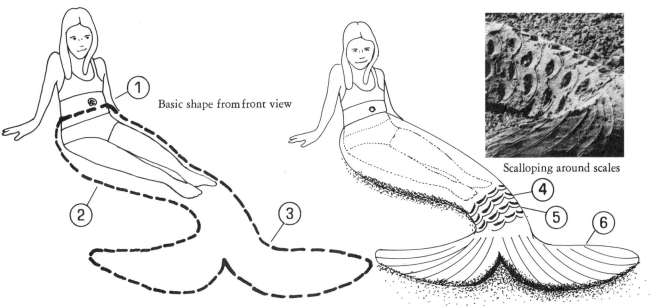

Basic shape from front view

Scalloping around scales

Seahorse (lying in sand)

Suggested size: 8 feet long, 2 feet wide, 6 inches high (in relief).

Distinguishing features: Curved body, curled tail end; bony bumps create saw-toothed pattern; tubular snout.

Making the outline

Mark off length of seahorse.
Draw an outline. See top view.
Clear sand from around outline.

Sculpting the body

1) With hands and putty knife, shape tubular snout.

2) Using shovel, make saw-toothed pattern all along sides. See photos.

3) Pressing sand between hands:
   a) Repeat saw-toothed pattern within body as shown.
   b) Make ridges along body and tail, lining them up with points of saw-toothed pattern.

Adding the feature

4) *Eye:* Form circle slightly larger than a soda or coffee cup lid. Mound up; add lid, pressing into place.

Final touches

Undercut around head.
Rake background sand.
Add water or await tide for dramatic effect.

Guide to tools and decorative materials

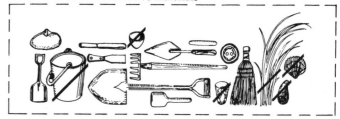

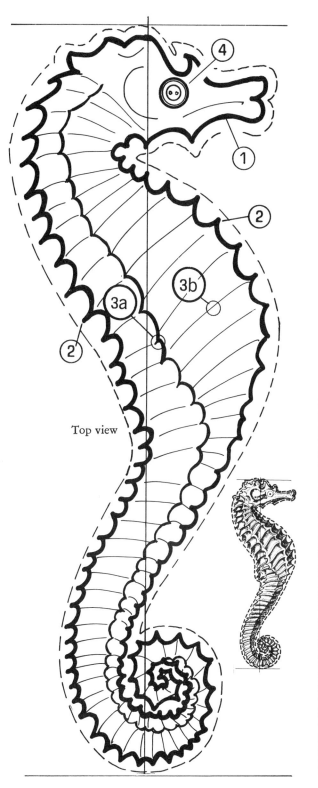

④

①

②

③b

③a

②

Top view

Shark (full-bodied/head and "jaws")

While photos and drawings are for jaws as well as the entire creature, instructions are for jaws only. We think you'll have fun with that.

Suggested size: 2½ feet long, 2 feet wide. 3 feet high.

Distinguishing features: Pointed snout; evil eyes; five gills on either side of head; large, crescent-shaped mouth; two rows of sharp, jagged teeth.

Making the outline

1) Draw a large circle.

Sculpting the body

2) Pile up shovelsful of sand; sand will naturally form conical shape.
3) With hands, widen head at eye level.
4) *Mouth:* With pointed tool, etch outline. Cut into mouth, and remove sand from center of mouth to suggest openness.

Adding the features

5) *Teeth:* Insert broken clam shells into mouth. See photo.
6) *Eyes:* With trowel, cut out small ledges where head widens; press in mussel shells.
7) *Gills:* Etch curved lines on sides.

Final touches

Undercut all around.
Leave background rough; add mounds of powdery sand to suggest foaming water.
Sprinkle powdery sand on sides and back.
Rake sand away from back to create illusion of wake.

Optional: Dorsal fin behind sculpture. See photo.

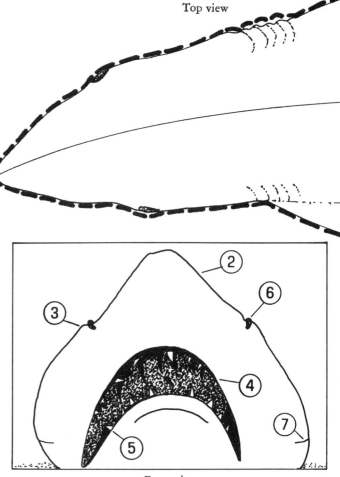

Top view

Front view

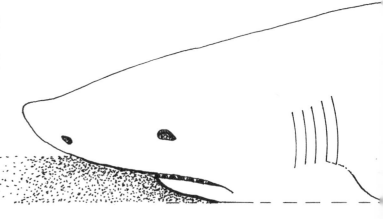

Guide to tools and decorative materials

Turtle

Suggested size: 3 feet long, 3 feet wide, 18 inches high.

Distinguishing features: Top and bottom shells; symmetrical pattern on top shell; four flippers (legs), neck, and short, pointed tail all emerging from between the shells; turtles move on flipper tips.

Making the outline

Mark off length of turtle.
Draw an outline. See top view.
Clear sand from outline.
Begin mounding.

Sculpting the body

1) Mound the body and make smooth all around.

2) With hands, mound up neck/head and flippers.

3) Add sand to form short, pointed tail.

Adding the features

4) *Shell pattern:* With putty knife, form scalloped edges of shell; with trowel or fingers, outline growth rings on top shell; remove sand from between outlines (or set in clam shells instead).

5) *"Raised" head:* To give raised effect, undercut head and neck by angling putty knife down to remove sand.

6) *Shell separation:* With putty knife, remove sand to define points at which flippers, tail, and neck emerge.

7) Undercut belly and legs to separate bottom of turtle from sand. *Caution:* Do not cut in too far or sand will crumble.

Final touches

Smooth and firm all over.
Add small pebbles for scales on legs, tail and neck.

Guide to tools and decorative materials

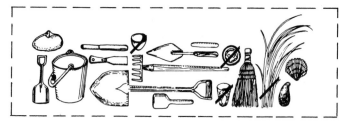

Basic shape from side view

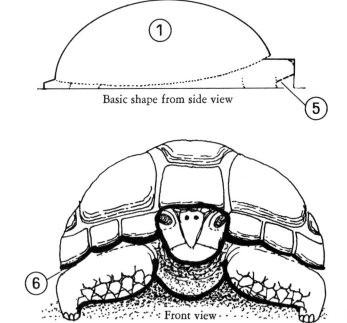

Front view

36

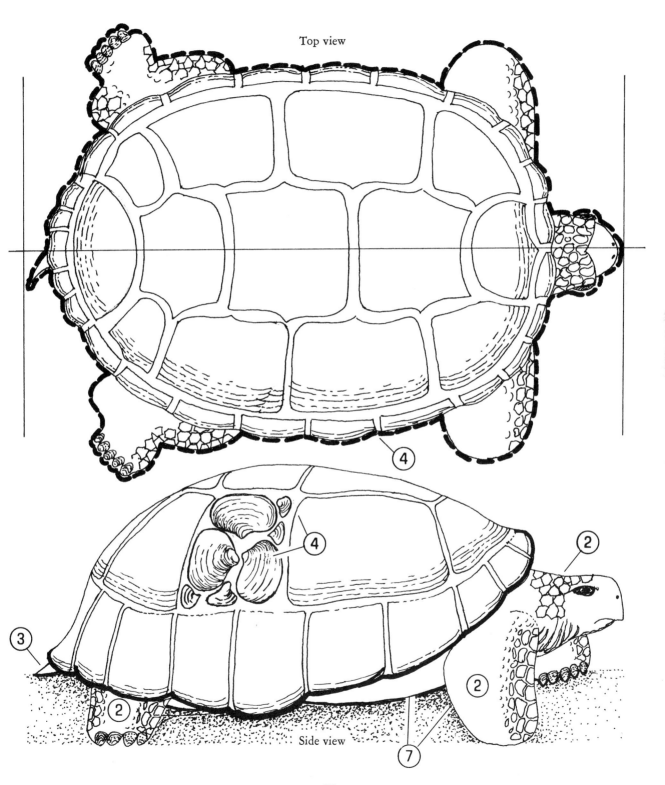

Top view

Side view

37

Walrus

Suggested size: 6 feet long, 6 feet wide, 3½ feet high.

Distinguishing features: Large, fat body with wrinkled skin; four flippers; tusks, extending from mouth like teeth; whiskers.

Making the outline

Mark off length of walrus.
Draw an outline. See top view.
Clear sand from outline.
Begin mounding.

Sculpting the body

1) Mound sand up high at front; taper down to rear.
2) With hands, round and firm head.
3) With hands or shovel carve sand away to form chest; make firm.
4) Mound up front flippers high and round at shoulders.
5) Extend flippers out from body and rest on sand base.

Adding the features

6) *Eyes:* Push in mussel shells.
7) *Nostrils:* Add mussel shells.
8) *Mouth:* With sharp tool, etch outline.
9) *Tusks:* Roll up two pieces of newspaper; push up carefully into corners of mouth; "glue" with wet sand for additional support.
10) *Whiskers:* Push grasses or straws into sand around mouth.
11) *Five o'clock shadow:* With sharp tool, make small holes between nostrils and mouth.
12) *Ridges on flippers:* With sharp tool, etch in five bony ridges on each flipper.
13) *Wrinkles:* With sharp tool, etch all over, especially at joints.

Final touches

Firm and smooth all over.
Undercut all around except at tips of flippers.
Rake sand all around.

Guide to tools and decorative materials

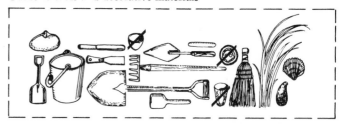

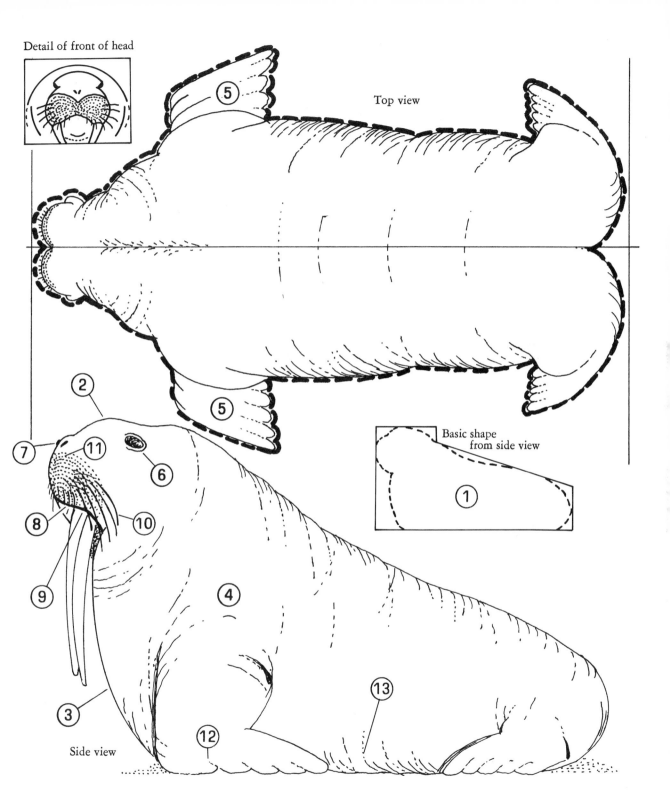

Detail of front of head

Top view

⑤

⑤

Basic shape
from side view

①

②

⑦

⑪

⑥

⑧

⑩

⑨

④

③

⑬

⑫

Side view

39

Whale

Suggested size: 10 feet long, 2½ feet wide, 2½ feet high.

Distinguishing features: Massive, rectangular head; side flippers; flukes or tail; wide mouth, extending around sides of head; blowhole (nostril).

Making the outline

Mark off length of whale.
Draw an outline. See top view.
Clear sand from outline.
Begin mounding.

Sculpting the body

1) Mound up sand for body, tapering downward toward tail.
2) Mound up tail.
3) With hands, mold flippers.
4) Undercut, especially in tail area, so it appears lifted.

Adding the features

5) *Mouth:* With sharp tool, etch outline.
6) *Eyes:* With putty knife, cut sand away for eye area above mouth; insert small white shells as eyes; into these place smaller black shells as *pupils.*
7) *Eyelids:* Etch in small curves.
8) *Blowhole:* With trowel, dig small hole; insert long grasses and/or soda cup full of water for illusion of water spout.
9) *Ridges on tail:* Etch with putty knife.

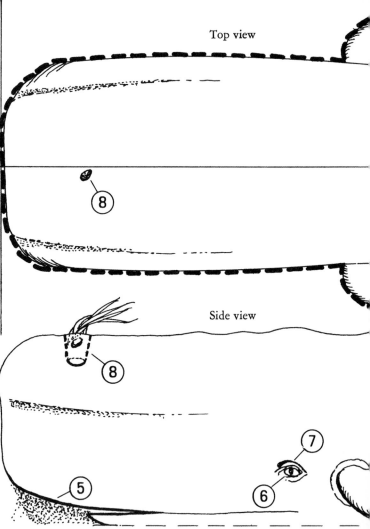

Top view

Side view

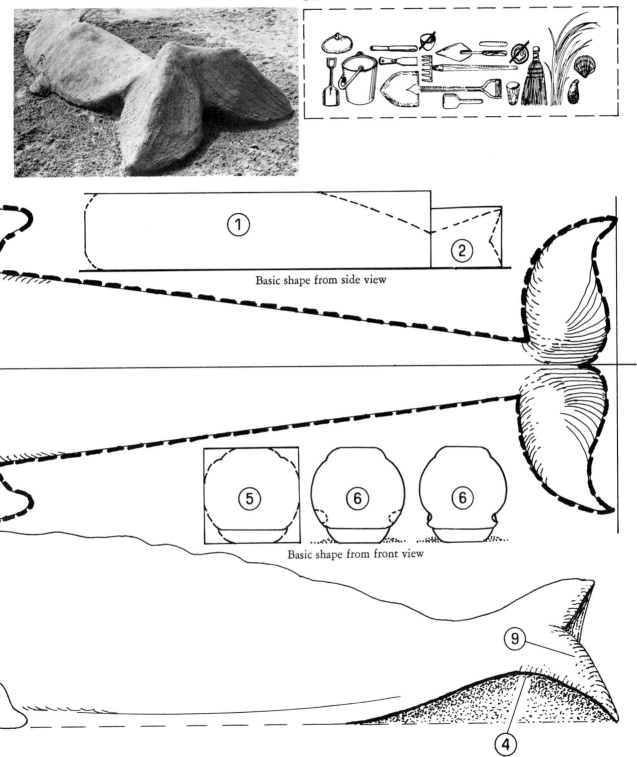

Guide to tools and decorative materials

① ②

Basic shape from side view

⑤ ⑥ ⑥

Basic shape from front view

⑨

④

Castles

Throughout the ages, every country has had fortresses of one kind or another, from the walls of Babylon and Jericho in ancient times to the elaborate stone castles of Europe. Whether occupied by conquerors, kings, fairy princesses, or robber barons, the castle has always been a symbol of power.

For protection, castles were usually built on a naturally defensible site—atop a steep hill or on a spur of land extending out into the sea. Further defenses were such obstacles as a ditch or moat around the outer wall, an additional encircling wall, a portcullis—heavy, iron-spiked gate which could be dropped quickly at the entrance—and towers in the outer wall from which to take aim against attackers. The "keep," a structure located in the middle of all the defenses, was where the lord of the castle lived.

The design often depended on the type of attack a castle was required to withstand. Mining was a favorite method of "breaching"—or breaking through—a wall. This involved digging a deep hole outside the castle which led up to and under the castle wall. A fire set at the far end would travel through the tunnel by way of wooden supports and bring the wall down. To thwart this type of attack, the castle builders added a sloping skirt or "batter" of stonework at the base of the towers and the wall. In time, round towers replaced square towers. These enabled the castle's protectors to keep watch on every spot around the outer wall. The development of gunpowder in the 1400s caused further modifications—lower walls and wider ramparts to support cannons.

Castle designs are many and varied. Following are a few types of castles, each with a brief history and step-by-step instructions for building it in the sand. Most of the castles are still standing. The instructions are accompanied by simplified ground plans and drawings. (Photographs are of the actual castles on original sites in the thought that it is preferable to have the ideal as the model.) You can see all the de-tails and recreate as many or as few of them as you like. The castles appear in order of complexity—easiest ones first—but none of them is too difficult to make. They all require patience and a steady hand.

How to build castles in the sand

Make the castle large enough—at least two feet long or in diameter—so that you can get at the details with your hand and putty knife. Most of the same techniques used for sculpting sand creatures apply to sculpting sand castles. Slight modifications may be called for. For instance, if you build your castle on top of a hill, mound the hill first, then level a large area on top of the hill and draw your outline there. For the detailed parts, work from the center out—so you won't knock down what you have already finished. Keep the castle courtyard neat by removing loose sand before erecting the wall. Dig the moat and build the drawbridge last. (The builders of real castles dug the moat and built the high outer wall first in order to work on details in relative safety.)

Dripping

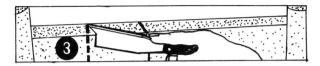

Dripping very wet sand and building it up by degrees produces a "fairy tale" type castle. For this, the sand must be quite wet, almost the consistency of molasses. Because you need plenty of water, either make the castle near the water, or dig yourself a little hole to use as a reservoir. You may discover additional uses for this "drip sand" technique.

Towers and walls

Use molds to construct towers of uniform size and shape. A plastic mold containing several heights and shapes can be bought for under one dollar wherever beach supplies are sold; tapered soda cups make good small towers and sand buckets make larger ones.

You can also mound up the sand and model it with your hands, using a putty knife to define the edges.

Towers were usually set into the walls, projecting half outside and half inside. Build up the wall between the towers in the same way ridges were made for the seahorse, i.e., laying up sand against one hand with the other or by applying the flat edge of a trowel or putty knife first to one side, then the other. To give your castle architectural detail, clearly define the point where the tower meets the encircling wall. Do this by inserting the point of a trowel or the blade of a putty knife in the angle, moving it gently out in one direction and then the other.

The tops of the towers should be at least one story (or one-third again the height of the wall) above the ramparts (to allow the archers to take aim against the enemy scaling the wall). Crenelations—the notched edges at the top of the wall or tower—can be cut out with a sharp tool.

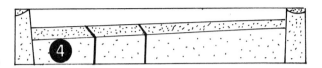

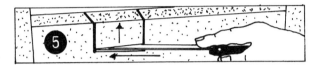

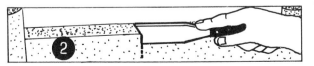

Basic steps in cutting crenelations

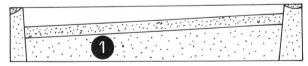

Moats and drawbridges

Dig a moat around the base of the castle wall or around the mound on which it is built. Note in the castle drawing that a platform or "berm" usually extends out from the wall before the incline to the moat begins.

Don't be afraid to build a sand bridge across the moat. It's fun. But don't make the span very long. Proceed cautiously. If the bridge collapses, build the mound up and try again. For the more timid castle builder, an easy, reliable way to make a drawbridge is to lay a popsicle stick, or any sticks, across the moat. Fill the moat with water or wait for the high tide to do it for you.

A good time to take a picture of your castle is in the late afternoon when the sun casts shadows of the towers and the wall into the moat and onto the sand.

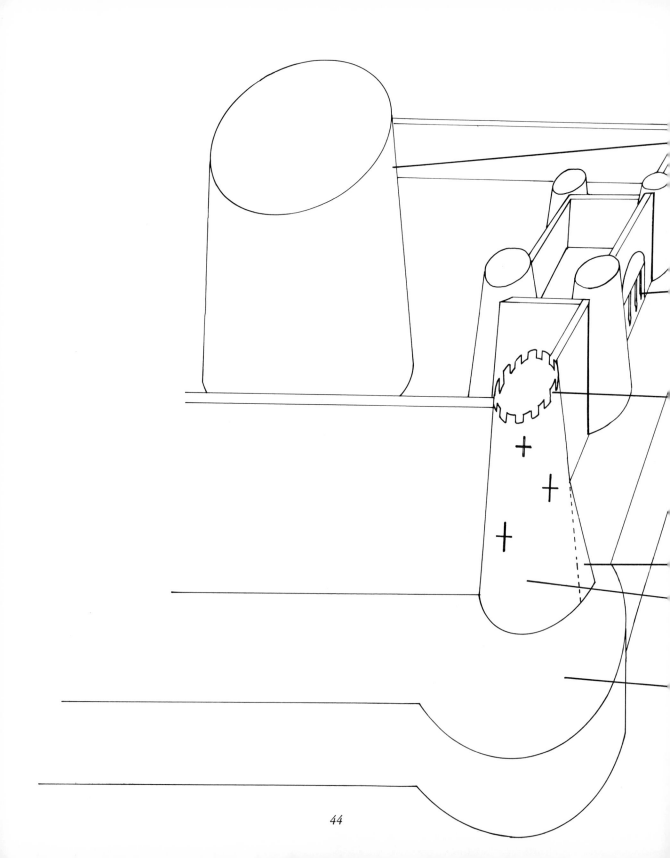

44

Castle Details

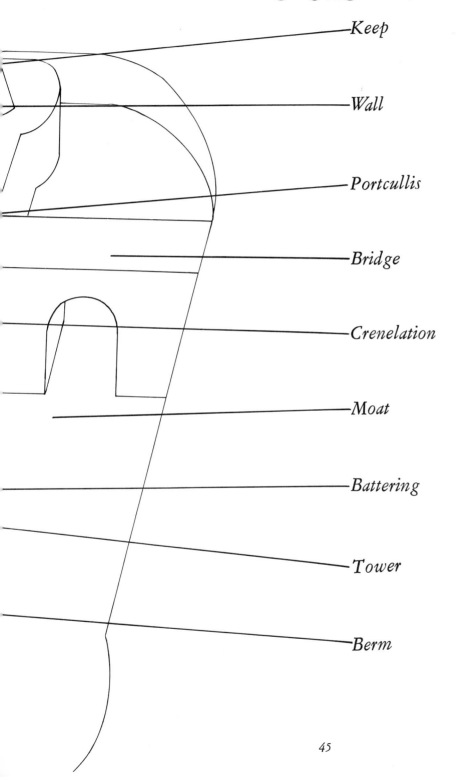

Keep

Wall

Portcullis

Bridge

Crenelation

Moat

Battering

Tower

Berm

Mont St. Michel (as a "drip" castle)

Pictured here is the real Mont St. Michel on its rocky island off the coast of France. It looks very much like a drip sand castle. Abbey buildings dating from the fourteenth century occupy the top of the mount with the church's spire rising at the center. A small village at the base of the rock is surrounded by a fortified wall. Formerly isolated at high tide, the island is now connected to the mainland by a causeway.

The drip castle shown here is based on the general shape of the real Mont St. Michel. Any building with spires provides an attractive silhouette and lends itself to the drip castle technique. Is there a hotel or church nearby whose outline you would like to reproduce in the sand?

The style is free form. You have to work fast and race against the waves. The sand must be very wet—like syrup—so choose a site near the water's edge. The advancing tide will enhance the effect of your drip castle.

Drip Castle

1) Lift up a handful of water-soaked sand.

2) Holding hand over site, dribble sand through open fingers while raising and lowering arm. Raising forms high, narrow peaks; lowering forms low, thick peaks. Sand will naturally build up drip upon drip; you can go as high as you wish.

3) To create additional spires, continue to work quickly, repeating motions with wet sand until desired heights and shapes are achieved.

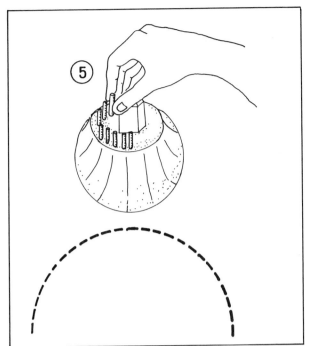

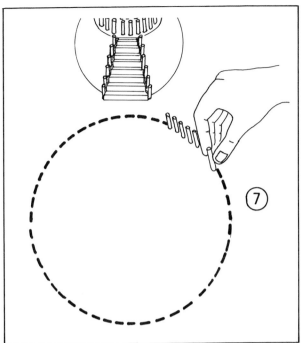

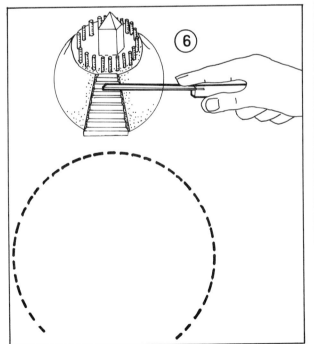

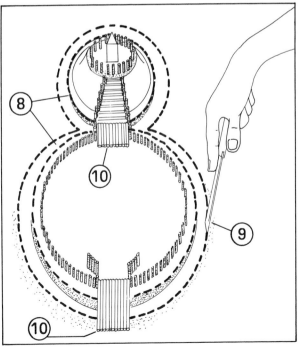

Harlech

Harlech Castle, in Wales, was the northern outpost of a defense system ordered by Edward I of England to hold Wales once it had been conquered. The ruins of the castle still stand on a rocky bluff above sand dunes, but when it was built in 1290, the sea washed over the rocks and provided natural protection. Harlech is a concentric castle, that is, there are two encircling walls—a low, outer wall and a tall inner one with round towers set into it. The outstanding feature of Harlech was its impenetrable gatehouse with four towers, two portcullises and "murder" holes above the entrance through which to shoot at intruders. It was such a massive, well-protected fortress that it was never taken by force, only surrendered when the defenders were in danger of starvation.

Preparing the site

1) Pile up shovelsful of sand to form a mound on which castle will stand. Flatten top.

2) On top of mound, etch ground plan of castle as seen in top view. Note location of four corner towers and four gate towers.

Making the towers

3) Empty pail or plastic mold filled with sand over etched locations to form towers. Trim with putty knife to desired shapes.

4) To add conical roof shown in drawing, but not in photo: Use hands or a funnel the same diameter as mold used for tower.

(Continued)

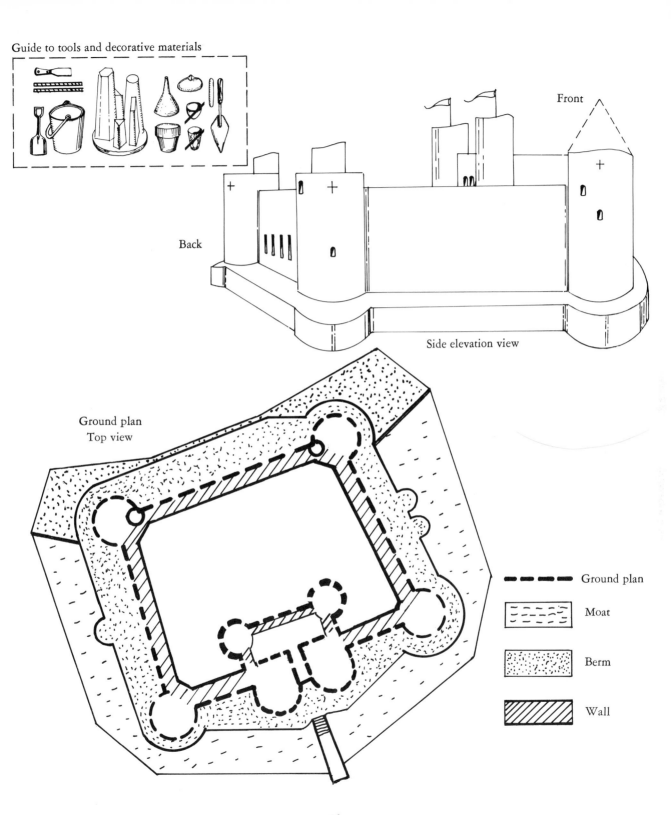

Guide to tools and decorative materials

Front

Back

Side elevation view

Ground plan
Top view

- - - - Ground plan

Moat

Berm

Wall

Harlech *(Continued)*

Making the walls

5) With hands, build up castle walls. Connect walls to towers. Build up interior gate walls. Connect them to gate towers.

Making the moat and drawbridge

6) Etch outline of berm or platform all around castle.

7) To define bank, and for moat at base of berm, follow outline and dig straight down with putty knife.

7a) To define opposite bank of moat use putty knife to etch outline and dig straight down.

8) Remove excess sand to begin forming trench for moat.

9) Clear away sand in trench.

10) With hands, build up a drawbridge connecting gate entrance with opposite bank.

11) Make a tunnel in drawbridge to allow water to flow through.

Final touches

Add water to moat.

Push twigs or straws into tops of inner gate towers as flag poles.

With putty knife, etch outlines of windows and crosses for openings through which arrows were fired.

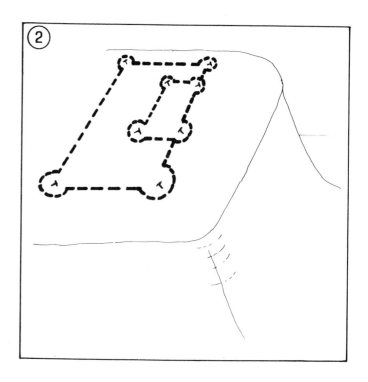

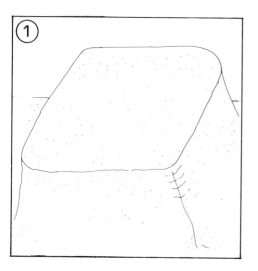

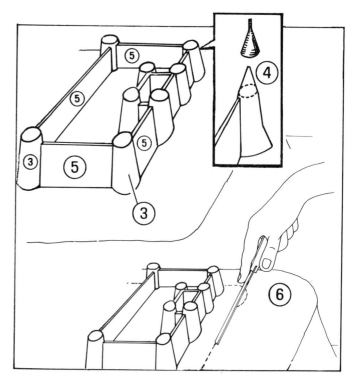

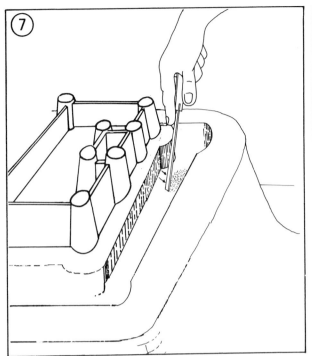

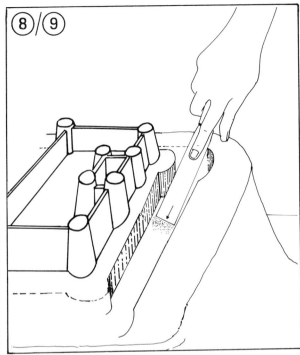

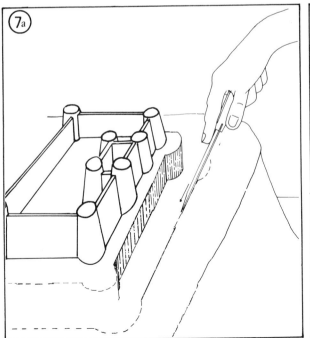

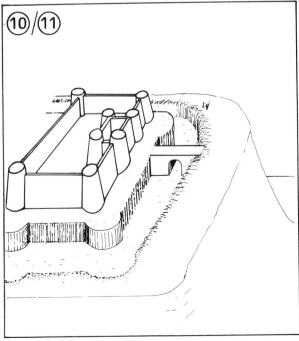

Deal

Deal Castle was built by order of Henry VIII in the early 1500s to guard the south coast of England. It represents the final stage in British castle design nearly 500 years after the first simple wooden forts were erected on earthen mounds. The low, sturdy walls are shaped like a double flower, each circle having six "petals." On the outer wall, there was plenty of room to mount artillery, while the enemy's cannon balls would be deflected by the rounded shape of the petals. Each petal of the inner wall had gunports to command the narrow space between the walls and protect the round keep in the center from attack.

This structure looks complex but it is not hard to build. It is largely platform upon platform.

Preparing the site

1) Outline circular ground plan.
2) Divide circle into six "pie slices."
3) Etch outline of six petal-shaped towers. See ground plan.

Making the towers

OUTER TOWERS

4) Fill pail or plastic mold with sand and form towers.
  4a) Cut off top halves; flatten.
5) Fill interior with sand.

INNER TOWERS

5a) Flatten as base for inner towers.
6) Etch outline of six inner towers.
6a) Form inner towers same as above, same height as outer ones.

CENTRAL TOWERS

7) Fill inner part of circle with sand; flatten.
7a) Etch outline for keep.
8) Fill pail with sand and form keep the same height as towers; flatten top.
9) With hands and putty knife, form six-sided tower on top of keep. Start with a tall, round shape and cut away to form six flat sides tapering upwards to a point.

(Continued)

56

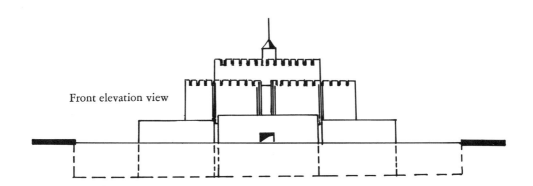

Front elevation view

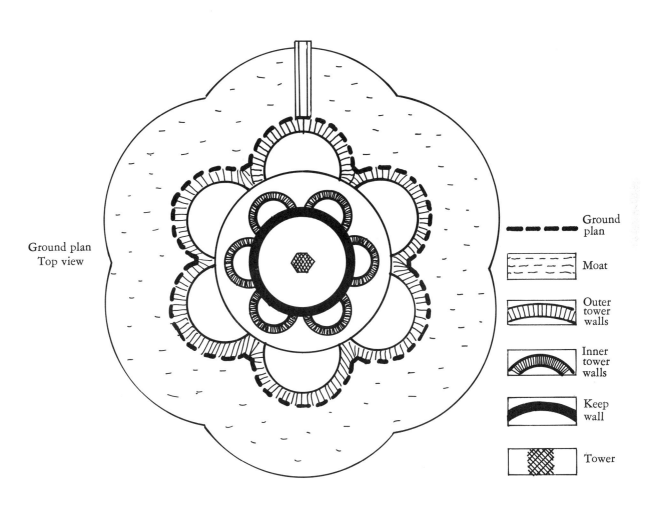

Ground plan
Top view

- - - - - Ground plan

Moat

Outer tower walls

Inner tower walls

Keep wall

Tower

Deal *(Continued)*

Making the walls

10) With hands, build up flat parapet or ledge on tops of towers.

11) With putty knife, make crenelations.

Making the moat and drawbridge

12) To form trench for moat at base of outer towers, etch shape shown by broken line and dig straight down with putty knife; clear sand away.

13) With hands, build up a drawbridge connecting gate tower with bank on opposite side of moat.

14) Make a tunnel in drawbridge to allow water to flow through.

Final touches

Add water to moat.

Push twig or straw into gate tower as flagpole.

Guide to tools and decorative materials

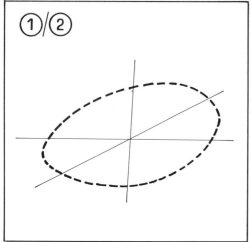

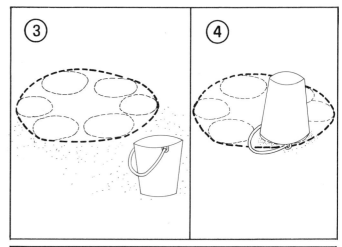

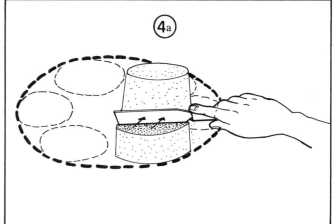

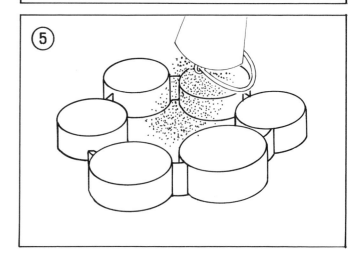

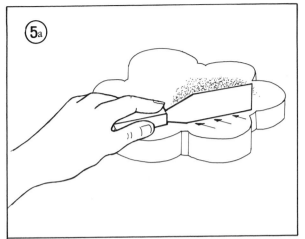

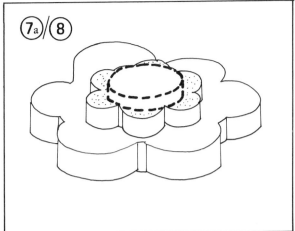

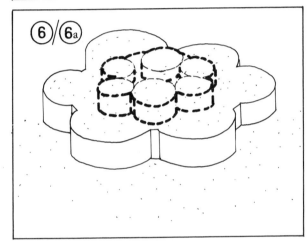

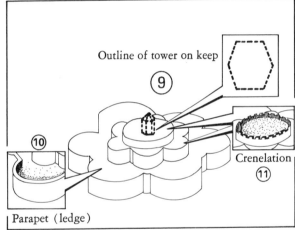

Outline of tower on keep

⑨

⑩

Parapet (ledge)

Crenelation

⑪

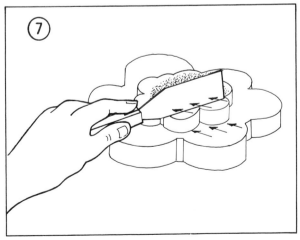

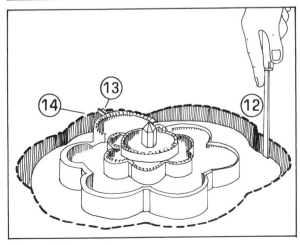

Krak des Chevaliers

The Krak des Chevaliers (castle of the knights), one of the most important strongholds during the Crusades from 1100 to 1271, still stands atop a hill in Syria. A reservoir between the two circular walls provided water for the castle as well as an extra line of defense. A mazelike entrance to the higher inner section deterred even the most determined attackers. The castle fell eventually, in 1271, only because of a trick: A forged letter from the Grand Commander ordering the knights to surrender. The natural protection of the steep slopes on three sides was a great factor in the defense of the Krak des Chevaliers.

Preparing the site

1) Pile up shovelsful of sand to form a steep mound; firm and flatten top.

2) On top of mound, etch outline of outer towers and walls. See ground plan.

Making the outer towers and wall

3) Fill pail or plastic mold with sand and form towers; use additional sand and/or cut away with putty knife to achieve varying bulk and shapes of towers.

4) With hands, build up outer wall connecting towers. See photos.

(Continued)

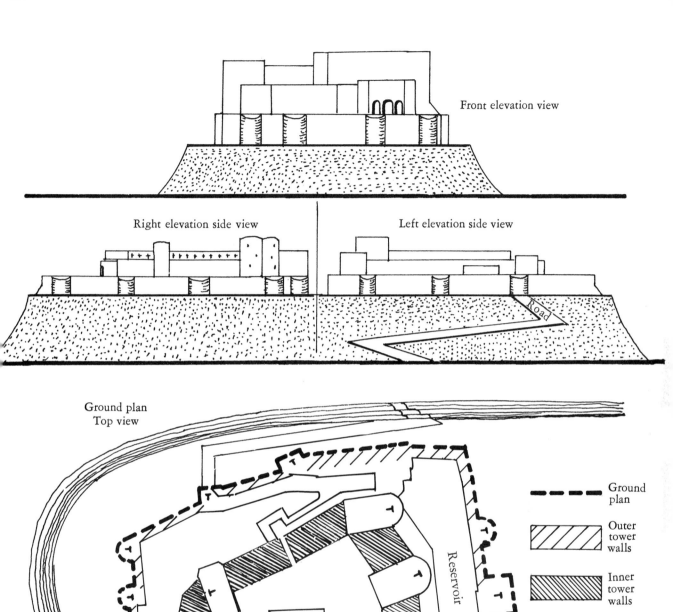

Front elevation view

Right elevation side view

Left elevation side view

Road

Ground plan
Top view

Reservoir

- - - Ground plan

Outer tower walls

Inner tower walls

T Tower

61

Krak des Chevaliers *(Continued)*

Making the inner towers and wall

5) Follow broken line and etch outline of inner towers and wall. ("T" indicates tower.)

5a) Fill pail or plastic mold with sand and form towers; use additional sand and/or cut away with putty knife to achieve varying bulk and shapes of towers.

5b) With hands, build up inner wall connecting towers. See photos.

6) Add battering to inner towers and wall.

Final touches

7) Etch in crenelations to tops of outer towers.

8) Etch in arches.

Form road along top edge of mound, winding down to sand base. (See drawings, page 61.)

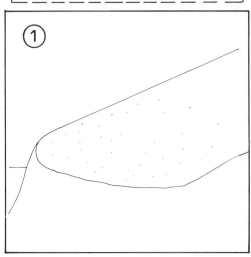

Guide to tools and decorative materials

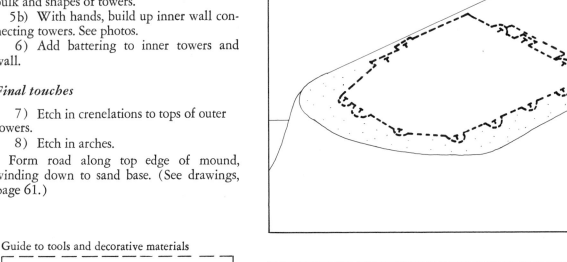

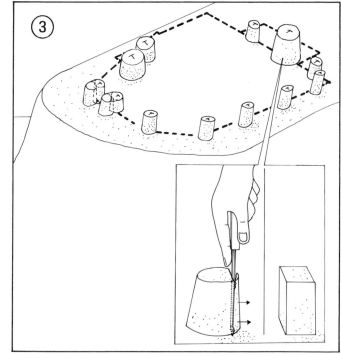

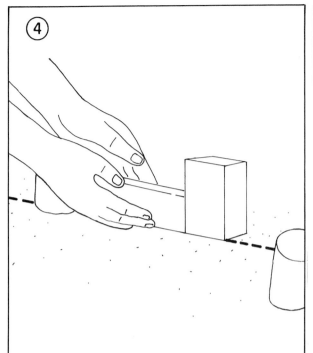

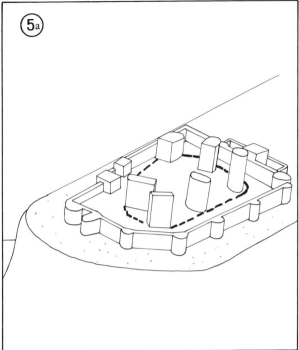

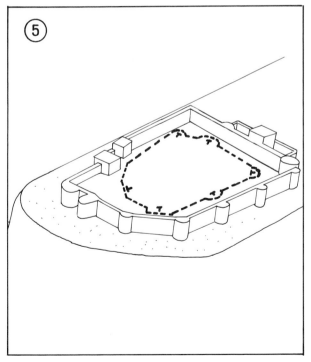

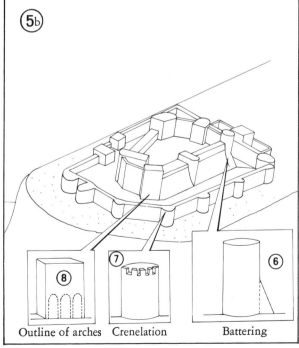

Outline of arches   Crenelation   Battering